RIDDLES

Challenging Brain Teasing Riddles For Kids And Adults, Stimulating Mind Growth For Fun

George Smith

Table of Contents

Introduction

We are a strange group, we humans. One of our greatest pleasures is to take something very confusing, and just for the sheer pleasure of doing so, making sense of it.

Riddles. Brain Teasers. Problems. Call them what you will, they give us hours of fun (or minutes, if we are really good at them). But it won't be a riddle to you as to why you bought this book (and thanks, by the way, for doing so). Once you get started you will find yourself absorbed into the mental gymnastics you need to solve these tricky clues.

And there are all kinds here, story riddles, logical problems, some short and some long, plays on words and even chapters of some famous riddles in literature…the list goes on. Not only do you have the fun of solving the problems, either alone or with your friends or family, but there is little more fun than setting problems for others to solve. Watch them puzzle over the answer, dropping in crucial clues when they are needed.

This book provides all of that fun. George Smith is a puzzle king, a person possessed of the sort of complex mind that thrills in finding the best riddles in the world *and* making up his own. The challenge for you is, can you solve his mysteries?

Perhaps yes, perhaps no, most likely some you will, and some might just need a sneak to the answers. Plus, chapters come with an example of the typical puzzle in that section, with a breakdown of how to apply logic to solve the challenge. Even beginners, the young, the old and the in-between, therefore, can have hours of joy with this collection.

So, wait no longer. Start with the first chapter, a nice easy introduction to some seriously mind-bending puzzles, and make a start.

Chapter One: Diddly Riddly

We are going to start out with a few easy examples to get your brains into gear. Here are twenty, still challenging riddles which can be taken as light warm up exercises before the serious work begins.

So, get your cup of coffee ready, turn off the TV, send the kids to Grandma, put the dog into kennels and here we go…

Oh, and by the way, each of the clues comes with a hint (not too obvious, and you'll soon get the idea) but if your mind becomes too entangled, the answers are at the end of the chapter. Good luck.

Example

The Growing Word

Which word becomes shorter when you add two letters to it?

Answer – SHORT

That is because the word short has two more letters added to make it into the word 'Shorter'. To reach that answer look at the question and think of all the different ways it could be interpreted. You are trying to think in a way that is not the normal method of thinking. Normally, we think of something becoming smaller when it gets shorter, but the question is a contradiction. Something cannot become shorter when it gets longer. Therefore, the question needs looking at from a different perspective. The key word is 'shorter'. The answer is to look totally literally. 'Shorter' is two letters longer than the word 'Short'. Switch the interpretation around, and the question is now: 'What does 'short' become if you add two letters to it?' We can see that 'shorter' is one possibility.

1

I'm easily broken and that's how I work.

The problem I have is that I'm only of use when I'm broken. It doesn't matter whether I am needed for my original task or as an important part of everyday life. Broken I am good, whole I am not.

And, to be frank, once I am broken, there's no fixing me.

If I am dropped, get the emergency services to scramble quickly.

What Am I?

2

The *Whole*-Hearted Object

If I were a t shirt, I'd be thrown in the garbage. Holes in the top of me, holes in the side of me, holes at the bottom and even in the middle. It is enough to make you wring my neck, but that would make me cry.

You'd think I'd leak everywhere, but I don't really.

What Am I?

3

No thing in the universe is comparable to me…

I am loved by humans more than life itself. When two lovers meet I am still a greater attraction. I am wanted by the richest people in the world, yet I am owned by the poorest. The meanest, tightest, most Scrooge like man in the world will still happily spend me, but the most generous, the most philanthropic would never consider giving me away.

When you have everything you could ever desire, you will still want me.

What Am I?

4

Always in a rush…

I am a bit rash, I admit. My brain always follows my actions. I get there first, then thoughts come closely behind.

.

And in getting to my destination I can run, but never walk.

What Am I?

5

Maybe lost, but never stolen.

I am always there – at night, I call unannounced, during the day, I disappear without warning.

I always make sense, but never do.

What Am I?

6

The Shy Object

I like the majority of me to stay out of sight, and although I am shy and retiring, I am also very dangerous when disturbed.

And, strangely, my whole is lighter than the parts that make me up.

What Am I?

7

I am extremely damaging but there's nothing to me.

Gosh, I am annoying. I can destroy objects and even lead to death. I can ruin your car, and make your house disappear. I swallow money. I can usually be clearly seen, which makes me only slightly less dangerous than when I am hidden. But, even though I can be as big as a crater, I am completely weightless.

When you add me to something, I make it lighter.

What Am I?

8

The strongest creature in the world.

Nobody can do what I do. It would break their backs if they tried.

Even though I am poor, I leave silver in my wake.

What Am I?

9

Something that cannot be restrained for long.

Nobody can keep me in. When I want to escape, I do, no matter how hard you try to stop me, I will win in the end. You will encounter millions of me in your life, in fact so many, that usually you will forget that I am there. But even though I might be insignificant, I am keeping you alive!

I weigh nothing but cannot be held back.

What Am I?

10

The Contradiction

I will run, but never walk, I need my bed, but never sleep on it. I have a head, but never think, and my mouth is wide, but never talks.

I am always born in the Spring.

What Am I?

First Ten Answers

(Your score analysis is presented before the answers to help avoid spotting the solutions by mistake…)

9 to 10: Pure genius, your mind is able to think laterally and out of the box.

6 to 9: You have a riddling talent, and with more practice could become a mental master.

3 to 5: More practice needed but by the end of the book, you will be much better at these kinds of puzzles.

0 to 2: Never mind, it takes a while to master this way of thinking.

1)   An egg
2)   A sponge
3)   Nothing
4)   A nose
5)   Dreams
6)   An Iceberg
7)   A hole
8)   A snail
9)   A breath
10) A river

Riddle Some More

1

The Kingmaker

I make crowns, but not just for monarchs. I fill caves with gold and build bridges of shining silver. Even though you might not like it, one day you know you will need me.

You fear me, even though I help you.

What Am I?

2

A ball game?

As ball games go, I am a bit of a disaster. The thing is, you can catch me, but you can never throw me.

George Smith

Sadly, I am nobody's friend.

What Am I?

3

Making History

I make history. I am old, and young. Everything has me.

I can certainly go up, but never come down again.

What Am I?

4

Can you find me?

Although you seek me, because I make you purr, you will not find me in hiding.

In fact, seek me in the centre of Paris, or perhaps at the end of the Eiffel Tower. I both begin and end the river, but never get wet, and although I start every race I never reach the finish.

If I join a fight, I make it scared.

What Am I?

5

The Victim

Beat me, crush me, tear at my skin – it will be you that cries, not me.

I will probably one day be executed; and have my head chopped off.

What Am I?

6

I am the GREATEST!

13

Trees, flowers, beasts, birds. The earth, the planets, the skies and the universe. All live in my control. I speed away and cause you regret when you are happy. Yet I last forever. I am everywhere, yet invisible. Everything is created under my watch, yet I have no form.

I am so omni-powerful, yet you can carry me on your arm.

What Am I?

7

The cup doth floweth over me.

I crack and pour. You can find me at the end of a bunch of tulips. I am mostly responsible when someone falls on ice. But only at the end, and never at the start.

I seem to be forever joined, yet can be separated with just one word

What Am I?

8

The Invisible Presence

I am all about yet cause a storm when I arrive. You can capture me, but not hold me. I can destroy houses yet weigh nothing. You hear me, but I make no sound.

I am in us all, and it is rude to let me out.

What Am I?

9

A Short Life

Doing my job kills me, wastes me away, but still I do it. I hate the wind and am better fat than thin.

I am light, but can be heavy

What Am I?

15

10

The Perfect Murder Weapon

I can kill like a knife and will never be discovered. I am cold hearted. I am beautiful. I am a spear that never rusts.

I glitter and shine but cannot be put in jewellery.

What Am I?

Answers

9 to 10: Brilliant, especially if this is better than your last score.

6 to 9: Fiddling with riddling has made your more than middling.

3 to 5: As Paul McCartney once said: 'Getting better all the time.'

0 to 2: Still taking too many wrong paths.

1) *A dentist*
2) *A head cold*
3) *Age*
4) *The letter 'r'*
5) *An onion*
6) *Time*
7) *Lips*
8) *The wind*
9) *A candle*
10) An icicle

Chapter Two: A Tonic For Logic – Riddles Requiring Lateral Thinking

In this section you will find ten lengthier but logical riddles. Read the story carefully and then try to use logic to work out what has happened.

There is an example below of a well-known riddle of this kind, plus some guidance as to how to reach the answer. This logical approach can be used for the other riddles.

Example

The Riddle of the Elevator

Every day Mr. Brown follows the same routine. He gets up and has a shower. He turns on his coffee machine, puts some sourdough in his toaster and pours himself some juice. He takes in the view from his kitchen window, looking out at the hills in the distance, over the freeway that can just be heard when the wind is blowing in the correct direction. He eats his breakfast – strawberry jam on Sundays, raspberry for the rest of the week, then heads off out of his apartment.

He walks along his corridor, saying hello to Mrs. Bernstein if she is leaving as well (they usually bump into each other) and makes his way to the elevator. He calls it, steps inside (if Mrs. Bernstein is with him, he lets her go first) and descends to the ground floor lobby.

He steps outside, and admittedly here his routine might change. He waves goodbye to Mrs. Bernstein and then, any day Monday to Friday, turns left to head to work. On Saturdays he crosses the road and goes into the gym. On Sundays, he turns right and heads to the store that sells his favourite blackcurrant flavoured toffees. They are a treat just for Sunday.

When he returns from his daily chores, he enters his apartment building and calls the elevator. He enters and ascends to the fourth floor. He then exits the elevator, turns left to the staircase and climbs some flights of stairs, after which he crosses the corridor and enters his apartment to enjoy the rest of his day. The only exception to this routine is on the occasional day when he returns at the same time as Mrs Bernstein. On those occasions, they go in the elevator together, and enjoy a little chat outside her door before he returns to his own home.

Why does Mr Brown follow that routine?

Answer

As with all good riddles, there are red herrings as well as crucial information in the story. A part of the skill is to work out what to eliminate and what to keep.

Let us take each piece of information in turn, and see if anything jumps out at us as being unusual:

He gets up and has a shower. *Nothing too interesting here. Mr Brown is not dirty, he has a bathroom, but none of that is unusual.*

He turns on his coffee machine, puts some sourdough in his toaster and pours himself some juice. *Again, nothing too unusual* *here. He appears to be a man of routine, which might have significance. Hold that information.*

He takes in the view from his kitchen window, looking out at the hills in the distance, over the freeway that can just be heard when the wind is blowing in the correct direction. *OK, that does tell us something. If he can see the hills and the Freeway, he must have a decent view, and that implies he lives high up.*

He eats his breakfast – strawberry jam on a Sunday, raspberry for the rest of the week, then heads off out of his apartment. *A man of routine, once more. A fondness for raspberries?*

He walks along his corridor, saying hello to Mrs. Bernstein if she is leaving as well (they usually bump into each other) and makes his way to the elevator. *He is a sociable person.*

He calls it, steps inside (if Mrs. Bernstein is with him, he lets her go first) and descends to the ground floor lobby. *Nothing too much here. Mr. Brown is a polite man. He uses the lift to get from his floor to the exit of the building.*

He steps outside, and admittedly here his routine might change. He waves goodbye to Mrs. Bernstein and then, any day Monday to Friday, turns left to head to work. On Saturdays he crosses the road and goes into gym opposite. On Sundays, he turns right and heads to the store that sells his favourite blackcurrant flavoured toffees. They are a treat just for Sunday. *There doesn't seem too much here that links to the final question, but once more we see a man of habit, who saves his treats for a Sunday. Might that be relevant?*

When he returns from his daily chores, he enters his apartment building and calls the elevator. He enters and ascends to the fourth floor. *The first really interesting thing. Why would he go* *to the fourth floor? Is that where he lives? Does he visit someone on that floor?*

He then exits the elevator, turns left to the staircase and climbs some flights of stairs, after which he crosses the corridor and enters his apartment to enjoy the rest of his day. *So, he goes straight to his apartment, but climbs some stairs to get there.*

The only exception to this routine is on the occasional day when he returns at the same time as Mrs. Bernstein. On those occasions, they go in the elevator together, and enjoy a little chat outside her door before he returns to his own home. *Again, the notion that he is a gentleman comes through, but also that he goes to the correct floor when he is not alone. That means the problem does not lie with the elevator.*

We then have to use this information to deduce why he goes all the way down in the elevator, but only some of the way up.

Does he like the exercise? Seemingly not, because he starts off in the elevator, and he walks to work and goes to the gym. Is there a fault with the elevator? Again, it would seem not because it is able to go down, and that means it must go up to reach his floor. When he is with Mrs Bernstein it works.

That suggests that the reason he conducts this strange ritual has to do with him rather than the elevator or apartment block. He is a gentleman, he appears to only know Mrs. Bernstein, he is a man of habit. He does not go out much socially. In all likelihood, he is man who keeps to himself. Somebody who does not ask for help or advice. Somebody who resolves his problems himself.

But the elevator is clearly significant. Let's think about an elevator for a moment. A box, usually with a door close button, and buttons to the floors the device serves. Imagining twenty floors, they are usually presented starting with the lowest, the ground floor or basement, then go up the wall of the lift one or two floors at a time.

Mr. Brown goes to the ground floor, whose button is low down, but gets out at the fourth floor, which is on a lower button than the tenth floor. A small child would not be able to reach the button for a high floor. Let us imagine Mr. Brown lives on the twelfth floor. He cannot reach up to that button, and being a self-contained man, doesn't ask for help. Therefore, he reaches as high as he can, the button to the fourth floor, and walks the rest of the way. But, when Mrs. Bernstein is with him, because he knows her, he allows her to reach for the button, so he can travel all the way up in the elevator.

Thus, the reason for Mr. Brown's behaviour is that he is severely vertically challenged and doesn't like to ask for help.

That works, and if it works, it is right.

1

The Motorcyclist

It is a barren landscape, the desert that lies between two countries in an unnamed part of the world. Simeone is the border guard at the break in the long chain fence that marks the borders between these far-off nations.

His job is quite boring, so when a man arrives on a motorbike one day, he is interested. He examines the man's bike, and it seems normal, if new and shiny. However, on the back is a large bag that seems almost to be riding with the driver, whose name is Miguel.

Simeone asks what is in the bag. "Sand", comes the reply.

But when there is desert in both directions as far as the eye can see, why would a person take sand across a border? Simeone decides to investigate. He orders the bag to be opened, and searches for hidden drugs, cash or jewels. But he finds nothing. He investigates the motorbike once more, but all seems normal. In the end, after checking Miguel's papers, he waves him through.

The following week, at the identical time, the same thing happens once more. But again, Simeone can find nothing untoward in the bag of sand, or the bike. This continues for most weeks for the rest of the year. Simeone is deeply suspicious but can find nothing wrong.

Over the years, Miguel will ride up the border from time to time, the bag of sand on the back of his bike. The two become almost friends. Then, one time, it is Simeone who has something to say. 'I am retiring tomorrow, this is the last time you will pass through my border,' he says.

Miguel is sad and offers to take the customs officer out for a meal to celebrate his retirement. The two discover they have much in common, and the meals become a regular occurrence. Then, one day, when their friendship can stand the test, Simeone asks the question that has unsettled him for years.

"My friend," he says, "I was a good customs officer. I caught many smugglers in my time. But so often you would bring bags of sand across my border. You must have been taking something across. Please, tell me, what was it that you were smuggling in the sand?"

"Ah", replied Miguel with a smile...

What was it that Miguel was smuggling?

2

The Scattering

A young couple in love were walking through the fields. One spots some broken pieces of wicker scattered over the grass. They think it is strange but move on, arm in arm. A little while later they come across a picnic basket, with plates and mugs and chicken legs spread around the area.

Mystified, they move onwards again, and next come across some blankets, then a box of tools. Even though they are heading for the beautiful, steep hills that lay ahead, they stop to investigate but cannot work out how the litter appeared.

As they get closer still to the hills, they see a pile of clothes spread along the field, a coat, then a jersey, some shoes, then a shirt and even some trousers. But suddenly, the mood takes a turn for the worse and matters become macabre because there, laying on the floor, is the almost naked body of a man. His legs are broken, and the couple are sure that he is dead. By now, they are almost in the shadow of the hills, and a dark gloom has spread over the landscape.

But, as they kneel down beside him, the injured man opens his eyes.

'What happened?' asked the couple.

What explanation did the injured man offer?

3

A True Story

The following tale is a little dark, and tragic in its way, but it is also true. Rather than just a riddle, this is a genuine mystery that faced Australian police a few years back.

The coastline around the southern end of that enormous island turns, within a mile or two of heading inland, into huge, beautiful forest. But such is the heat, the dryness and the omnipresent wind that, from time to time, terrible fires break out. Although the Australians try to halt the progress of these deadly disasters, once they have taken hold, they become almost impossible to stop.

So it was on the occasion in question. Vast areas of former forest were turned into ash, the withered stumps of recently great trees all that remained of the green and verdant land. The environment is self-preserving, and will grow back over time, but police and the authorities knew that many animals, and sometimes people, become caught in the fire's path, and when that happens there really is no escape.

So, when they investigated, it was with the fear that they would come across some victims.

And, one day, a body was discovered. Sadly, the person had perished, but was covered in a strange blackness, which seemed to have become almost a part of his or her bones. The body was far away from roads, from houses, from paths. It was just there, in a burnt out clearing of what had recently been densely packed forest.

Can you explain what the police had found, and how that strange result came to pass?

4

Emergency Operation

A man and his son decided to have a cycle ride in the countryside. It was a beautiful day and they had travelled far away from town when disaster struck. A truck rounded the corner of the narrow road too quickly, lost control and struck the two cyclists. The driver was horrified to see what he had done and phoned the emergency services. Two ambulances arrived, and one collected the father, the other took the son. Since they were mid-way between two towns, each of which had a small hospital, the ambulances took the injured to different hospitals.

When the son arrived, he was quickly assessed. It was clear that he was not in any mortal danger but would need an operation.

He was prepared, but when he arrived in the operating room the doctor said: "I can't operate on you. You are my son."

How is this possible?

5

The Vital Question

After a long and generally good life, an old man dies. It is not as bad as he fears, and he travels along a bright white road until he reaches a junction. In front of him is a wall, and a corridor leads both left and right. Three people, dressed in white, stand in front of him. The eldest one stops the man and says the following words:

"You lived a long life and in it you did some good things and some that were bad. Now is your judgement time. To the left is one door, and to the right is another. One door leads you to heaven, where all the pleasures of the universe will be yours. The other takes you to hell. A dark, fire filled furnace in which pain and terror will be your constant companions.

"You must decide which door to open, and once you have made your decision, you cannot change your mind. But because you have been mostly good, you have an opportunity to guarantee what your future holds. You may ask one question. But not of me, of my angels. Beware though, because one these angels will always tell the truth. The other will always lie. Remember, just one question. Ask it wisely."

And with that, the speaker vanishes. The man is left in front of the two angels, who are identical and offer no hint of which is which. But the man always enjoyed puzzles. He thinks for a moment, then approaches one of the angels. He asks a question which guarantees he will know which door will lead to heaven, and which to hell.

What question does the man ask?

6

Get Rich Quick

A man is sitting in a bar. His is nursing his glass of beer because he knows it is the last he will drink for a long while. Because, you see, the man is very poor. So poor, in fact, that he has no money at all.

He is sitting there, feeling down, when another man comes into the bar. He produces his wallet and orders a bottle of champagne, flashing $100 bills.

The poor man looks on and has an idea.

"Do you like a gamble?", he asks the rich man.

"Of course," says the wealthy one, "How do you think I earned all my money?"

"OK, I have a special skill," replies the poor beer drinker. "I know a song for every girl's name in the world. You give me a name, and I will sing you a song with her in it. It will be a genuine song. You will even know it. If I succeed, you give me all the money in your wallet. If I don't, I will be your servant for the rest of the month."

The rich man accepts the bet.

"I have a cousin called Philomena Wolfson Sidebottom," he says.

The poorer man thinks for a moment. Then he begins to sing.

Soon, he is leaving the bar much richer than he entered it.

What song did he sing?

7

The Challenge of the Garbage Can

A new game show pilots on TV. The winner reaches the final where he is confronted by three large screens. Behind one of these screens is the star prize, a brand-new Jaguar. Behind the other two are garbage cans full of litter.

The final works like this. The contestant chooses one of the three screens. The host then reveals what is behind one of the other two. The screen drops away and there is always a garbage can. Nothing else can be seen.

The contestant now has a choice. He or she can stick with the screen they have selected, or they can swap to the other screen.

What is their best strategy? And Why?

8

The Farmer's Lot

A farmer needs to get some of his farm animals and products across the river to the other side and to his big barn. Unfortunately, the bridge is down, and the river is too deep for his tractor.

He does have a tiny boat, but it is only big enough to hold him and one of his objects.

He hasn't planned his day too well because his three items are his sheepdog, one of his chickens and a bag of grain.

His problem is that if he leaves the dog and chicken together, the dog will chase the chicken away. If he leaves the chicken and the grain together unattended, the chicken will eat the grain.

He puzzles for a moment, then has a moment of brilliance.

How does he get all his items across the river without losing any of them?

9

Dangerous Driving

A man is waiting on the sidewalk in Darksville, the blackest town in the country. In that forsaken place, the roads are painted black, the houses are painted black, even the sidewalk is painted black. The African man is wearing a black balaclava that covers his face, a long black coat, and black trousers. His shoes and socks are black. He has black make up on his eyes, which are closed, and wears black gloves.

There is no moon and the streetlights are all broken. The town is filled with silence. The man steps into the road to cross it when a speeding black car with headlights off screams around the corner. A collision seems inevitable, but at the last moment the car swerves out of the way and a catastrophe is avoided.

How did the driver know to swerve?

10

The Best Fieldsman?

It is a still day. A strong sports player is standing at the edge of the ocean, up to their knees in the water. There is no wind, no birds, no boats and nobody else around. The sports player is carrying a normal tennis ball and facing out to sea. The ball has nothing attached to it. The next landfall is thousands of miles away. In front of the player are miles of sea and behind yards of beach. The nearest house, wall, hill or whatever is barely visible on the horizon.

The sports player takes a breath and throws the ball as far as they can. They wait a few seconds, and then, without moving, catch the ball. It is perfectly dry, and the same ball as was thrown.

How is that possible?

Answers

7 to 8 correct – brilliant logical deduction.

4 to 6 correct – well done, these were hard, and you scored well.

0-3 correct – don't give up hope yet.

1)   *Miguel was smuggling **Motorbikes**. The sand was simply a ruse to distract attention from his main purpose.*

2)   *The first thing the man said was probably, "Help". But after that, he was able to explain what had happened. He was a member of a party who were **riding in a hot air balloon**. The hot air control developed some kind of fault, and it was obvious that the balloon would continue to lose height and crash into the hills it was approaching. Something needed to be done to keep the balloon in the air. The pilot decides that the only chance is for one of the passengers to jump out of the balloon and take their chances. He breaks off bits of the basket and they draw straws to see who will have to jump out. A loser emerges, but they try to give him the best chance of survival by throwing out all the spare equipment in the balloon. Finally, they even throw their clothes overboard. It is not enough, and the man **jumps out of the balloon,** which is low enough for him to survive. That is sufficient to keep the balloon above the hills, and it heads on to safety.*

3)   *This is a genuinely true story. One of the ways the authorities try to put out forest fires, which are normally close to the coast, is to fly helicopters which have huge grabbing tanks hung below them. They fly over the sea and scoop up thousands of gallons of sea water, which they then drop onto the fire in an attempt to slow it down and put it out. The incident in question occurred when the helicopter scooped up*

*a **scuba diver** with the water and dropped the diver onto the fire with the water. Very sadly, the diver was killed, and his body was then burnt in the fire. The rubberised wet suit he was wearing melted in the heat.*

4) *The doctor was the boy's mother.*

5) *The man can approach either of the angels. The question he asks is,* **"Which door would your friend say I need to go through to get to heaven?"** *The man then goes through the* **other door.** *The reason is that if he asks the TRUTHFUL angel, he will be told that the other angel would identify the door to hell, and send him through that, because that angel always lies. If he is asking the LYING angel, then he knows that the answer the angel gives will be a false one. In either case, the door indicated will be the door to hell, so he will go through the other one.*

6) *This is one of the easier ones. The man sings the most famous song in the world.* **'Happy Birthday.'**

7) *Mathematically, it is best to **switch** his choice to the other screen. This is for the following reason: when he made his first selection, he had a random one-in-three chance of being correct. That is because he chose one of the three screens. That meant that the other two had a combined probability of two in three. Now he knows which of those three **DOESN'T** hide the car, that better probability now lies with the other screen.*

8) *He does it like this. Firstly, he takes across the **chicken.** That leaves the dog and grain, which will remain untouched. He heads back and then collects the **grain.** He drops off the grain and takes the chicken back in his boat. Next, he takes the **dog** across. When he has finished his journey that leaves the dog and the grain on one side of the river, and the chicken on the other. They are all safe. He then goes back and collects the chicken.*

9) *It does not matter that everything is black, because the time is **mid-day** and there is lots of sunlight.*
10) *The sports player throws the ball **upwards** into the air and just waits until it falls down again into their hands.*

Chapter Three: *Riddling* Away From Trouble - Wordplay

In this section we have an alphabet of riddles. And there's the first clue. Here's a silly example to give you an idea.

Example

Which fruit always comes in twos?

Answer

Think of the different types of fruit, and as you come up with them see if the word has, or sounds like, a second meaning.

*Then, when you reach **Pear**, you see that a **Pair** means two of something.*

1

Which vegetable makes Arthur cough?

2

What is the name of the only everlasting fruit?

3

What do you call a girl who is good at transporting things?

4

What's the most popular name on an oil rig?

5

Which job begins with an E but starts with N?

6

Which type of boat is the nicest?

7

Which animal is best at math?

8

What do you call a road in the sky?

9

What name do you give to a digital truck?

10

Young Mr Time barely manages to make class. What is his first name?

Answers

9 to 10: Alphabet soup for you.

5 to 8: Scrabble-ing around for the answers?

0 to 4: Perhaps 'word work' might be a better phrase than 'word play'.

1) An **arti-choke**
2) A **bananananananana**
3) **Carrie**
4) **Derek.** *Work it out!*
5) An **engineer**
6) **Friend**ship
7) A **g-raph**
8) A **high-**way
9) An **i-Van**
10) **Justin** *(Justin Time)*

Another Set Of Commandments (or, The Next Ten)

1

Which US Secretary of State was known as being the most romantic?

2

What do you call someone who falls off a cliff?

3

What do you call a clever Scottish nut?

4

Name a boy who cannot stand.

5

What do you call an eight-legged cat?

6

What do you call a boy who enjoys swimming?

7

Where in Australia do the Royal Family live?

8

Which bird do you find in prison?

9

Which room in your house is the hardest working?

10

Which country sells the smartest clothes?

And A Bonus Six, So No Letter Feels Left Out

11

On a cow, which teat provides the most milk?

12

Who is the richest woman in the world?

13

Which US state asks the most questions?

14

Name a man who is no more. (Hint: You should see right through this one!)

15

Which colour do you shout when you drop something on your toe?

16

Which religion is the top?

Answers

12 to 16: Cryptic Crossword!

7 to 11: Easy Clues.

3 to 6: Wordsearch.

0 to 2: Scrabbler – Junior version!

1) *Apparently **Kissing-**er was quite a lover-boy.*
2) *Clearly, a **ledge-end***
3) *Mac-Adamia*
4) ***Neal***
5) *An **octo-puss***
6) ***Paul***
7) ***Queens-**land*
8) *A **Robin***
9) *The **Study***
10) ***Thai-**land*
11) *I don't know, but if your luck is like mine, it will probably be the **udder** one.*
12) ***Val U Ball***
13) ***Why?** Oming*
14) *He is an **Ex-Ray***
15) *You **Yell 'Ow!'***
16) ***Zen-**ith*

Chapter Four: What Am I

What Am I? riddles are some of the most popular of all. Again, we start with an example to help those who are not familiar with this type of puzzle.

Example

I sound like one letter

But in me you'll find three.

There's two letters in the word

And another two in me.

I sound like a pronoun

But I'm blue, brown or grey.

I'm the same at each end,

And the same either way.

What am I?

We need to thank laterally and literally about every line and begin to pull together common ideas.

I sound like one letter – *we can start by thinking which letters sound like a word. Bee, Sea and see, Gee, Eye, Oh, Pea and Pee, Queue, Tea and Tee, You, Why.*

But in me you'll find three. – *so probably a word with three letters that sounds like one letter. That narrows the possibilities down a little. But not much! Bee, Sea/e, Gee, Eye, Pea/e, Tea/e, You, Why.*

There's two letters in the word – *that line disagrees with the idea that there are three letters. What might it mean? Perhaps two* **different** *letters, which means one letter will be repeated. We can test it out and see whether the theory takes us to the answer. We now have Bee, See, Gee, Eye, Pee and Tee.*

And another two in me**. –** ***A hard line. Could 'I' have been stung, with two bees, do I see with*** *two eyes, I have two eyes.*

I sound like a pronoun – *do any of the words we have left sound like pronouns? Yes, the word* **Eye** *sounds like* **I. I** *is a pronoun. Maybe there is the answer. Now we can confirm it.*

But I'm blue, brown or grey. – *Yes, eyes can be those colours.*

I'm the same at each end, - *Yes, the word ends and begins with the same letter, so it could be said to be the same at each end.*

And the same either way. – *Yes, the word reads the same forwards and backwards.*

The answer is *Eye.*

Riddles

1

You will need to measure me

For my life to be known,

And I know that you'll miss me

When I have flown.

What am I?

2

On a bright sunny morning

You know that I'll appear

I will lay at your feet

I will always be near.

You can run, you can hide

But you won't lose me.

Until the clouds fill the sky

And the sun you can't see.

What am I?

3

I make you laugh, I make you cry.

I make you stamp your feet.

I make you happy, I make you sad

And at times I will make you weep.

I am loud, I am quiet

I get you out of your seat.

I am master, I am boss

Everyone runs to my beat.

What am I?

4

Every day begins with me

And at dusk I'm the first thing that you'll see.

I make daisies grow and daffodils too

Dave knows me well…but you'll never guess who.

What am I?

5

I have a skin

I have eyes

I have a beautiful jacket.

So why do people want to mash me up?

What am I?

6

With the sharpest teeth I lie in wait

And black and white and red – I still seal their fate.

The bloodless victims lay in wait

To be ever placed in a conjoined state.

What am I?

7

It can cover your body

But it is not clothes.

And the more that it's used.

The smaller it grows.

What is it?

8

Flat as a pancake

Round as a ring

Has lots of eyes

But can't see a thing.

What is it?

9

I am two faced, but people still desire me.

I am literally worth nothing, but people still collect me.

There are so many of me, but people still steal me.

I cannot speak, but phrases come from me.

What am I?

10

I lay low between my taller neighbours.

Take away my beginning and my neighbours come closer together.

Take away my end twice, and I become everything.

What am I?

Answers

Those were quite tough questions. We have included explanations for some of the trickiest examples.

8 to 10: excellent riddling.

4 to 7: middling riddling.

0 to 3: fiddling riddling.

1) **Time** *(time only exists when it is measured. Time flies when you are having fun.)*
2) **A shadow** *(a shadow only appears in sunlight. It lies at your feet and follows you around. You cannot lose it until the sun disappears.)*
3) **Music** *(they are all things people do when music plays.)*
4) **The Letter D** *(all the key words begin with the letter D.)*
5) **A Potato**
6) **A stapler** *(well done if you got that one! A staple is shaped like a mouth with gappy sharp teeth and lives in the stapler. Paper is covered in ink which can be black, paper is usually white and there is a play on the word red and read. The stapler 'stabs' the paper, which being inanimate has no blood. It joins the paper together.)*
7) **Soap**
8) **A Button**
9) **A coin** *(a coin has two faces, by itself it is worth nothing, but it represents value. There are billions of coins in existence, but thieves rob people of their money. Another use of the word is in the phrase 'to coin a phrase'.)*
10) **A Valley** *(take away the first letter and it becomes 'alley'; take away the final two and it becomes the word 'all'.)*

Chapter Five: Random Riddles

Here we have ten random riddles using the styles we have seen already, with some variations. Warning – they are pretty tough!

1

A weighty problem

Forwards I am heavy, but backwards I am not.

What am I?

2

A dangerous friend

I am black, then red, then grey

And that's the point you throw me away.

I keep you warm and snug

But…never give me a hug.

What am I?

3

A private matter

If you have me, you can never share me

If you share me, you can never have me.

What am I?

4

The key, but not to the door

To understand me requires a key.

Not a key made by a locksmith. Not a key on a map or graph.

A key that only I will understand.

What am I?

5

Generations?

I walk on four legs in the morning, two in the afternoon and three in the evening. Late at night I might not have any legs.

What am I?

6

Am I even worth a dime?

There are three different ways of spelling little me

The first is a smell, quite heavenly

The next is some cash, from the small money tree

The third's what happened, when at my door it did be

I am many in just one, a one, two and three

What am I?

7

Is this my kind of town?

What a strange and windy place I am.

I am three sevenths of a chicken,

Then two thirds of a cat.

My end is half a goat.

What am I?

8

Don't make me whine...

I am made of five letters, and can be crushed, skinned or simply eaten.

Lose my first letter and I am field of crops or a dreadful crime.

With the first two gone I become your distant ancestor.

And take my second and you will stare at me open mouthed.

What am I?

9

The best people

My first two letters make me a man

But add another and I turn female

Add yet another and I become a great man

But only when I am whole do I become a great woman.

What am I?

10

All of it? Or not?

This is a strange thing, because when you take away the whole, some remains.

What is it?

Answers

9 to 10: No problem.

5 to 8: Although they were a problem, you weren't!

0 to 4: Big problem.

1) *A ton*
2) *Coal*
3) *A secret*
4) *A code*
5) *A Person (if the day is a metaphor for life, we crawl at the beginning, walk in the middle, need a stick near the end and ultimately may be left in a bed or wheelchair._*
6) *The homophones scent, cent and sent.*
7) *Chicago*
8) *A grape*
9) *A heroine*
10) The word 'wholesome'

Ten More Riddles, Sitting on the Page

1

Air Crash

If a plane crashes on the border between the US and Mexico, and the passengers are mostly Mexican, where do you bury the survivors?

2

Bible Stories

We are familiar with the story of the Ark and the Great Flood. But, how many of each animal did Moses take on to his vessel.

3

Farmer's World

Mr Jones the Farmer has had a successful season in his orchard. He has twenty rows of pear trees with fifty trees in each row. If each tree in his orchard averages fifty pieces of good fruit, how many plums does he have to take to market?

4

Colourful Homes

There is a famous little seaside town on an island off the coast of Scotland called Balamory. The town is best known for its colourful houses, in lovely reds, blues and peachy pink colours.

If we could build that in the States we could use red bricks for the red houses, blue bricks for the blue houses, yellow bricks for the yellow houses and lilac coloured bricks for the lovely lilac houses. What coloured bricks would we use for the greenhouses?

5

Quick Exit

A man was pushed out of an aeroplane. He had no parachute, but managed to survive with no worse damage than a few bruises.

How was that possible?

6

Holding forth...

What can most people hold easily in their left hand but never in their right?

7

School Days

At an elementary school, forty pupils wore blue coats, twenty-seven wore red and twenty-nine wore black.

But using that logic...

How many wore green coats?

8

Calendar Crisis

If the day after the day before yesterday was Wednesday, and the day before the day after tomorrow is Friday, what day is it today?

(That will make your brain ache!)

9

Tall Man Tricks

A man is six feet tall. He holds a glass beaker above his head, with his arm stretched upwards. He lets it drop to the carpet and does not spill a single drop of water.

How did he manage that?

10

Spelling Bee

Which word is always spelled wrongly?

Answers

9 to 10: Well done, award yourself a Gold medal.

5 to 8: Good try, give yourself a Bold medal.

0 to 4: Oh dear, all you can have is a very Old medal.

1) *Hopefully nowhere, because you don't* **bury the survivors.**
2) *None – it was* **Noah** *who took animals into the ark.*
3) *None, but he did take 50000* **pears***.*
4) *You won't need bricks of any colour, greenhouses are made of glass.*
5) *The plane had* **already landed!**
6) *Their* **right elbow***.*
7) *That is a tough one.* **49 students** *is the answer. The pattern works with the letter A being worth 1 student, B =2, C = 3. Therefore GREEN = 7+18+5+5+14 or 49.*
8) *It depends on how you look at it.* **Today** *is always the day of the week that it is. But if you are sticking to the premise, the answer is* **Thursday.**
9) *The glass was* **empty!**
10) *Wrongly*

Chapter Six: Mathematical Mazes

1

Eggs For Breakfast

Two fathers and two sons sit down for breakfast. They love eggs, and each decide to have one for their meal.

They each eat an egg, and three eggs are consumed.

How is this possible?

2

The Lost Dollar

Three women decide to go out for a pizza. They each order a dish from the $10 menu. Jill has a Pepperoni; Julie decides on a Vegetable and Jackie goes for a Hawaiian. Each of the pizzas, as is said, costs $10. At the end of their meal, they hand the waiter $30, paying $10 each.

A short while later the waiter returns with $5. He explains that they have a deal on that day whereby if customers purchase two pizzas from the $10 menu, they get a third at half price.

After a quick discussion, they decided to keep $1 each, and give the waiter a $2 tip, thus accounting for the $5 they were given back.

But Jill is looking confused. "Where's the other dollar gone?" she asks.

Jackie explains. "There is no missing dollar. We paid $10 each, got five back from the discount offer, and split that $1 each and two for the waiter."

"Yes," Jill insists. "So, we paid $10 each and got one back, that is $9 each, right?"

The others nod in agreement.

"Then we gave the waiter a $2 tip, yes?"

Again, there is agreement.

"So," continues Jill, "We each paid $9, and three nines are twenty-seven. Plus, two for the waiter. Twenty-seven plus two equals twenty-nine, not thirty."

What happened to the missing dollar?

3

Family Matters

A couple have their first child. It is a boy. Soon they decide that they want a second child.

What are the chances that they will have a second boy?

4

Chain Link

A chain is nailed to a wall. The chain is ten feet long, and its centre drops five feet from where each end of the chain is nailed to the wall.

How far apart are the two ends of the chain?

5

Making Things Add Up

There are only three positive numbers that reach the same sum whether multiplied together or added together.

What are they?

6

Hanging on the telephone

If you multiply together all the numbers on your telephone keypad...

What is the total number you reach

7

In Training

A woman suffers from severe claustrophobia. She has to catch a train for an important meeting, but knows that as it leaves her station, it enters a long tunnel.

Where is the best place for her to sit?

8

The Smoking Gun

A homeless person is severely down on their luck. They have few pleasures, and one of the ways to cope is to collect cigarette butts and use these to make new cigarettes. The homeless person knows that he needs four butts to make one cigarette.

He searches the streets and comes up with 16 butts.

How many cigarettes can he make?

9

Where's Waldo

A boy draws his own picture of Where's Waldo on a piece of paper. It is a good one, and when he gives it to a friend they insist that Waldo is not there, and it is a trick.

How can the boy prove it is not a trick without giving the game away?

'This thing all things devours:

Birds, beasts, trees, flowers;

Gnaws iron, bites steel;

Grinds hard stones to meal;

Slays kings, ruins towns,

And beats high mountain down.'

10

Bookshelf

A bookshelf contains several books. Sally wants a particular one and can't be bothered to read all the titles.

Her friend tells her the book is fifth from the left and seventh from the right-hand end of the shelf.

How many books are on the shelf?

Answers

9 to 10: You have a touch of an Einstein about you.

5 to 8: You won't ever be short changed at the check-out.

0 to 4: Time for an extra math class?

1) *The key to this one is that one of the three men is both **a father and a son**. For ease, let's call the men Jim, Joe and Jack. Jim is Joe's father. So that is the first father. Joe is therefore Jim's son – son number one. Jack is Joe's son, so that is the second son, which makes Joe into Jack's father. That is father number two. Of course, this leaves Jim as Jack's grandfather, but that is not a relationship in the question.*

2) *What a mindbender, eh? The key to the answer is to ignore Jill's interpretation. In fact, the three women spent **$25** on food and **$2** on their tip. So, they spent a total of **$27.** They paid that with **$9** each. Three times nine is twenty-seven. Each of their $9 was made up of a **$10** note with **$1** returned.*

3) ***50%** or **one in two.** The fact that the first child is a boy is completely irrelevant to the chances of the second child's gender. Although, the clever among you might point out either of the following facts. Firstly, there are slightly more women than men in the world, so that makes the chance of it being a boy slightly less possible, about 49.5 to 50.5, Others with a scientific bent might observe that if their first child is a boy, it might mean that one or both parents are genetically more suited to producing boys, which would increase the chances of another male offspring.*

4) *They must be **together,** attached to the **same nail.** If the drop is five feet, which is half the length of the chain, then the other five feet of the chain must be found in the five-foot rise from the*

bottom of the dip. In order for this, all the drop must be vertical, as if there was some sideways movement, the drop could not be a length of five feet.

5) One, two and three. One of the numbers had to be a one, as otherwise the multiplication would far exceed the addition. Therefore, the sum of the other two numbers needed to be one more than the total when they were added together.

6) 0. A keypad contains a zero and any number multiplied by this will end up as a zero.

7) The best place for the woman to sit is **at the back of the train.** Being claustrophobic, she wants to be in the tunnel for the shortest possible time. As the train gathers speed as it leaves the station, it will be going faster when the rear carriage enters the tunnel compared to when the engine enters the tunnel. Therefore, the rear of the train will spend less time in the tunnel

8) Five. The sixteen butts can make four cigarettes. He can then **use the butts from these cigarettes to make a fifth.**

9) You **cut a hole in another piece of much larger paper.** Then you place this piece of paper over the original, and show he is there without revealing where he is on the page.

10) There are **11** books on the shelf. Two ways of working this out. Either, the book in question is occupying two positions (5th and 7th from each end) so although you might expect there to be twelve books, there are only eleven. Or, there are four books to one side of the relevant book, and six to the other. Four plus six equals ten, plus the book identified to make 11.

Answers

9 to 10: You are very clever or have read the book.

5 to 8: Perhaps you read the book and remember some of it.

0 to 4: If you did read the book, I suspect you didn't enjoy it. And if you haven't get down to the library or local bookshop quick.

11) Mountains (although, as we know now, they do grow with plate movement in the Earth, and shrink with erosion).

12) Teeth.

13) Wind.

14) Sun on the daisies.

15) The Dark.

16) Eggs, or an egg box.

17) Fish.

18) Fish on a little table, mat at the table sitting on a stool, and the cat has the fish bones.

19) Time.

20) As we saw at the beginning of the chapter, Bilbo's pocket contains Gollum's ring.

Chapter Seven: Potter Puzzles

The phenomena that is Harry Potter re-introduced books to a generation of young people. Their popularity remains as strong as ever, perhaps even more so with the successful films starring Daniel Radcliffe, Emma Watson and Rupert Grint.

JK Rowling was a struggling writer with not two pennies to rub together when she created the first books. Working in an Edinburgh café, The Elephant House (on George IV Bridge, near Greyfriars' Bobby if you want to visit the legendary place in the heart of this most beautiful and fascinating of cities) she would sit at a large round table (it is still there but you need to get your timing right as The Elephant House is always bursting with customers) making a cup of coffee last as long as she could, while writing.

JK Rowling solved the riddle of how to become the best paid writer in the world. But can you solve some of the riddles she put into her books? Numbers 1 to 4 are riddles set by JK Rowling herself in the books, numbers 5 to 10 are riddles that lead to answers from the series.

1

From Harry Potter and the Goblet of Fire

Come seek us where our voices sound,
We cannot sing above the ground,
And while you're searching ponder this;
We've taken what you'll sorely miss,

74

An hour long you'll have to look,
And to recover what we took,
But past an hour, the prospect's black,
Too late it's gone, it won't come back.

Come seek us where our voices sound,
We cannot sing above the ground,
An hour long you'll have to look,
To recover what we took.

2

From Harry Potter and the Goblet of Fire, given to Harry by a Sphinx – and you will have to read the book to find this, it is not in the film.

First think of the person who lives in disguise,
who deals in secrets and tells naught but lies.
Next, tell me what's always the last thing to mend,
the middle of middle and end of the end?
And finally give me the sound often heard during the search for a
hard-to-find word.
Now string them together, and answer me this,
which creature would you be unwilling to kiss?

3

From Harry Potter and the Sorcerer's Stone (Philosopher's Stone in the original, UK version)

"Danger lies before you, while safety lies behind,
Two of us will help you, whichever you would find,
One among us seven will let you move ahead,
Another will transport the drinker back instead,
Two among our number hold only nettle wine,
Three of us are killers, waiting hidden in line.
Choose, unless you wish to stay here for evermore,
To help you in your choice, we give you these clues four:
First, however slyly the poison tries to hide
You will always find some on nettle wine's left side;
Second, different are those who stand at either end,
But if you would move onwards neither is your friend;
Third, as you see clearly, all are different size,
Neither dwarf nor giant holds death in their insides;
Fourth, the second left and the second on the right
Are twins once you taste them, though different at first sight."

4

From the Sorting Hat

Oh, you may not think I'm pretty, but don't judge on what you see, I'll eat myself if you can find a smarter hat than me.

5

A Character

I am the entrance to Hogwarts

But no sound comes from my buzzer.

Who am I?

6

Fun and Games

What is the most expensive trench in the Harry Potter books?

7

Jealousy, tis a green-eyed monster...

What does Harry Potter have that Voldemort does not?

8

Tough Person

Which Harry Potter main character is part flesh and part metal?

9

Romance in the air...

Which Harry Potter character is fondest of the moon?

10

Lost in the Puzzle

I am where the angry monarch lives.

I am where Germans say no.

I am only 0.75 of the way to my destination…

But I would run through walls to reach my goal.

Where am I?

Answers

9 to 10: Quidditch champion

5 to 8: Nearly Headless Nick

0 to 4: Draco Lucius Malfoy

1) *They are the voices of mermaids.*
2) *A spider (spy-der)*
3) *Complicated answer here… in order: poison, nettle wine, a potion to move the drinker forward through black flames, poison, poison again, nettle wine and finally a potion to move the drinker backwards through purple flames.*
4) *The sorting hat is talking about itself.*
5) *Dumbledore (**Dumb bell door**)*
6) *Quidditch (**Quid ditch**)*
7) *A Nose*
8) *Herm **iron** ee (Hermione)*
9) *Luna Lovegood*
10) *Platform 9 and ¾ in Kings Cross Station*

Final Words

And so, many thanks for buying and reading this book. I hope that you have found the riddles and puzzles challenging and fun.

Now it is time to use the ones that you like best on your family and friends, leave them puzzling over the problems you set. I finish with two great puzzle games. They are ones you can play at dinner parties, over Thanksgiving lunch at a party or on a long car journey.

The first is called 'Holidays'. It works like this. You (or the person leading) decide on a pattern which others must follow to be successful. For example, if your name is Colin, you might name objects beginning with the letter C. You say: 'I'm going on holiday and I am going to take a cap.' The next person, let us call them Bill, has a go. He says: 'I'm going on holiday and I am going to take a picnic.' You tell him that he cannot. The game continues going round until either everybody has the answer, or most people have, and the others are not going to get it. It is important that you always follow the rule that you have set.

The links can be anything. Perhaps you scratch your nose when you speak, perhaps you use the initial letter of the name of the person going next, you decide on the complexity of the linking clue.

The second game isn't original but is such fun that it is worth sharing. The game is called 'Mornington Crescent' and was invented on a radio game called 'I'm sorry. I haven't a clue' in Britain. Mornington Crescent is an underground railway station near the centre of London which is only open on a couple of days a week, and then only at certain times.

The idea is to share tube stations until a person reaches Mornington Crescent. The game works best if there is elaboration. The fun is that there are no rules at all, and some of the players need to know this. The others, or those observing, will try to find a pattern to understand the game but there isn't one.

It works with any group of destinations – cities, roads, rooms in a house, train stations, cities I the world.

Here's an example played by the aforementioned, Bill and Colin. This version involves flying to various cities to end up in Seattle (and nobody wants to go there, do they?)

Colin: New York

Bill: Good start. Washington DC.

Colin: Chicago.

Bill: San Francisco.

Colin (quickly): Austin.

Bill: You've got me on the run. Ummm. Philadelphia.

Colin: Des Moines.

Bill: Ha. Boston.

Colin: Seattle.

Bill: NO!

The watchers will be desperately trying to find out what was going on. And that is the riddle.

So,

My First is in Egg, but not in bird.

My second starts engine, or maybe not

And my third is in duck, as you may have heard.

Now it's all over, as you'll probably spot.

The

End.

44266587R00050

Made in the USA
Lexington, KY
09 July 2019